SCHALK'S LITTLE BOOK ON FUNDAMENTALS

What every combatives and martial
arts practitioner should know but
almost never gets taught.

Schalk Holloway

ISBN FOR PRINT EDITION: 9798517780560
Imprint: Independently Published

Cover design by: Schalk Willem Holloway

Dedicated to all of those combative and martial arts practitioners that are truly seeking mastery.

ACKNOWLEDGEMENTS

A sincere thank you to Misters Terry Trahan, Jack Lee and Gavin Coleman for taking the time to proof read and help me tighten up what is already a concise treatment. English is not my first language. I speak it fairly well but I still think in Afrikaans. Your help and guidance is much appreciated.

CONTENTS

INTRODUCTION

The Oxford Dictionary defines the word Fundamental (usually Fundamentals) as "a central or primary rule or principle on which something is based." Fundamentals are primary in the sense that they are what is most, or of first, importance. Fundamentals are those principles on which everything else is built - they are the principles that lie underneath everything else that we do. As such, whatever the Fundamental leads to is of secondary importance; if the Fundamental is not executed correctly then whatever else the Fundamental is a part of will not be executed correctly either.

Before continuing, I would like to acknowledge, from a position of gratitude, that the first time I heard about the concept of Fundamentals was in a blog post written by Marc MacYoung. Although I can't remember too much about the article itself (I think it was around 2009 or so), conceptually it got stuck in my brain and I've been mindful of Fundamentals ever since. With mindful I mean both in my own practice of combatives as well as ensuring I also focus on and correct Fundamentals in my clients.

That said, let us consider striking as an example. Striking is a form of force application. One type of striking that we are all familiar with is what is called the impact blow. To simplify, a straight punch is one variation of the impact blow. The goal of the straight punch is to apply as much force as possible to the target. However, force is physics. It is generated, increased, optimised, and delivered through certain unchanging principles, or rather, Fundamentals. To increase the applied force I need to understand these principles and how to execute them well, in simple terms, to punch harder I need to execute the Fundamentals correctly.

It's impossible teach or motivate someone to simply punch harder - I can only help them to execute their Fundamentals better; better Fundamentals will assist them in punching harder. This train of thought applies to all facets of combatives or martial arts - striking, takedowns, joint locks, speed, accuracy, and even mental aspects such as learning and rapid decision making. Fundamentals are what is most important.

The sad fact in today's combative and martial arts landscape is that many instructors, rather than teach or integrate Fundamentals correctly, opt for trying to simply tell or motivate their students to, for example, punch harder. Imagine, for a moment, the instructor standing next to the student yelling at them to "come on, harder, punch harder." Even though this sounds very motivating it might only work if the student is already executing the Fundamentals correctly.

When we reflect deeply on the true nature of Fundamentals it should become apparent how important it is to understand and execute them well. It begs the question, though: "If they truly are that important why are they not fully explored and taught within training contexts?" Personally, I suspect it is due to two primary reasons.

Firstly, I believe it is related to the proliferation of traditional martial arts into combatives and/or combat sports during the last few decades. Traditional martial arts had many quality controls embedded due to the long periods of instruction required for both practitioners and aspiring instructors. As the fighting arts started to move away from the traditional arts these quality controls unfortunately were left behind.

Furthermore, as the desire and need for hyper fast training periods increased we also lost the qualitative effect that long periods of training had on practitioners. I don't think faster training times are inherently problematic - there are definite contexts in which it is required - I do however contend that it increases opportunity for neglecting the Fundamentals, the problem being compounded if the instructor doesn't have a good understanding of the Fundamentals him or herself (kindly note hereafter I have referred to any person primarily using the pronoun him).

Secondly, I believe that it has become too easy to qualify or act as an instructor in contemporary times. We live in an age that promotes the pursuance of subjective purpose as an ultimate life goal. It should not be difficult to see how this value of pursuing purpose, when combined with a zeitgeist of instant gratification, as well as a social media landscape that allows highly flexible and effective advertising options, can quickly lead to a drop in the quality of instructors and instruction. Whether paying for and legitimately completing a quick instructor's course, or simply deciding to start doing one's "own thing," the ease with which we can do so these days increases the opportunity for neglecting the Fundamentals.

And herein lies the purpose of this little book on Fundamentals: it is little in the sense that it means to offer a concise, easy to study and easy to assimilate, treatment on the topic of Fundamentals. Its aim, with a laser like focus, is on educating both the practitioner and instructor with the Fundamentals pertaining specifically to combatives and martial arts. Its goal is to assist the reader to not only sharpen up, but rather to excel, in all aspects of their fighting career.

May this book be of immense value, effecting unparalleled increases in performance, in both you and your clients.

PART 1

Takedowns

BASE

It is empirical reality that the human body has mass and that its mass has weight. Through the force exerted by gravity on mass, that is, its weight, this mass consistently either stays on, or will fall to, the ground. When this mass is in some way anchored to the ground, meaning it's not falling, it has what we call a base. The base consists of whatever elements are currently bearing the weight of the mass.

If we had to imagine a chair with four legs, it would be the four legs that made up the base. If we had to imagine a motorcycle standing still, with its stand out, it would be the two wheels and the stand that made up the base. If we had to imagine a lemon lying on the floor, it would the parts of the lemon touching the floor that made up the base.

In terms of the human body let's consider the following examples **(each with a sketch below):**

A man that is simply standing still. His base would be made up of his two feet.

A woman that is kneeling but with one knee up (half kneel position). Her base would be made up of the lower leg's toes and knee and the lifted leg's foot.

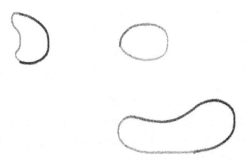

A child down on all fours. The child's base would be made up of both sets of toes, both knees and both hands.

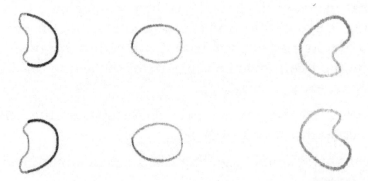

A man lying on his back with his legs in a bent raised position. His base would be made up of whichever parts of his feet, torso and arms are touching the floor.

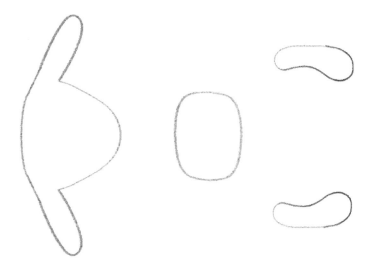

It's important to understand that the base relates to load bearing elements. If, in any of the examples above, one of the elements is touching the ground but not actually bearing load then it wouldn't form part of the base.

Furthermore, the base does not consist of the separate element themselves. Imagine drawing an imaginary line around the circumference of all the different elements. This imaginary line would be the base. **See our four examples but with the imaginary line below:**

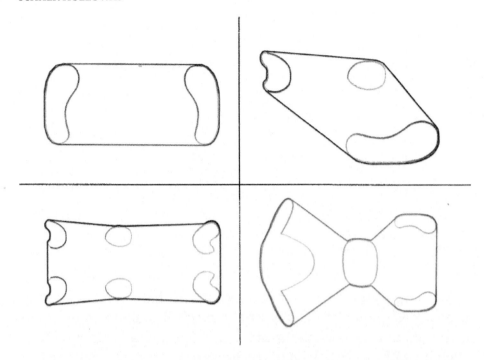

The two concepts above need to be brought together. If we, for example, had to take the man lying on his back with his legs in bent raised position, his base would be different if both feet were flat on the ground versus if one foot was only lightly touching (meaning it's not bearing load) the ground. **Note the difference in base in the two sketches below:**

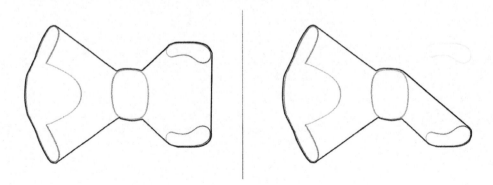

Now that we have a working understanding of the base let's quickly discuss the load bearing elements. For the purpose of this book, and as is customary in most martial arts, we will be referring to the load bearing elements in the base primarily as posts. Thus, whether it's a foot, knee, hand, elbow, head, or whatever other part of the body that's bearing load, we will refer to them all as posts. It just so happens, due to human anatomy and biomechanics, that the posts are usually the limbs and their respective extremities, but for our purposes we will call any load bearing element a post.

It's important to develop a consistent awareness of your own as well as your opponent's base, and as such, their posts. The location and management of a human body's center of gravity, in relation to its base, is the Fundamental dynamic when it comes to influencing a body's stability and subsequent balance. Being able to discern the current position and makeup of the base, whether through the visual or tactile sensory organs, is the prerequisite to affecting any takedown. That said, let's move on to a discussion on center of gravity.

CENTER OF GRAVITY (COG)

Gravity's direction of force is always downward (or towards the center of the earth).

All objects of mass have an imaginary (or hypothetical) position at which the combined mass of the object appears to be concentrated. Flowing from this position they also have what could be called a line of gravity. Imagine for a moment a line, with an arrowhead attached to the bottom, being hung from this hypothetical position. This line and arrow, when stationary, will be pointing towards the center of the earth. This imaginary line is what we call the line of gravity.

It's also important to note that this imaginary position, the center of gravity, does not necessarily have to lie within the object. The dimensions and distribution of the object's mass will determine where this point lies. However, due to the anatomical dimensions of the human body we can approximate a center of gravity for humans. This position, what we refer to as the COG, usually lies to the front of the second sacral vertebra. When facing the front of the human body we can imagine it to be an inch or two below the navel. If we had to draw a line from the second sacral vertebra to this front and below navel position, the COG would usually lie somewhere towards the middle on this line on what some refer to as the body's vertical axis. In general there is some variation between male and female due to differences in hip dimensions; specifically each and every human will have slight differences in this position due to variations in body shape, size, and proportions.

Back to the imaginary line of gravity. This line and arrow, when stationary, will also be pointing to the middle of the base as it's the base that is bearing the weight of the mass.

Notice these four principles of stability. Principles one to three have corresponding sketches:

1. When the base is large the object is said to be more stable as the line of gravity needs to move further for it to fall outside the boundaries of the base. As example consider a person down on all fours, weight evenly distributed between both hands, knees, and feet. It will be quite difficult to cause them to lose balance.

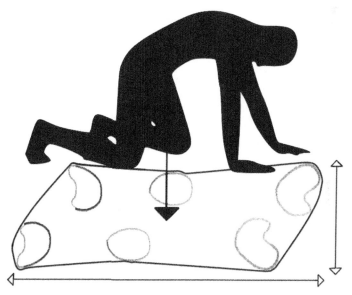

2. When the base is small stability will decrease as it becomes easier for the line of gravity to move outside the boundaries of the base. Here we can imagine a ballet dancer, feet together, raised on her toes. Should we trap her feet it wouldn't take much force to push her off balance.

3. When the base is wide but narrow, stability will increase in the wide direction of the base but decrease in the narrow direction of the base. Imagine the traditional martial artist in a deep horse stance. They would be able to manage a lot of incoming force on the line stretching form ankle to ankle, however, give them a firm punch on the chest and they will easily lose balance towards the rear. This principle also relates to stance integrity which will be discussed in more detail in the next chapter.

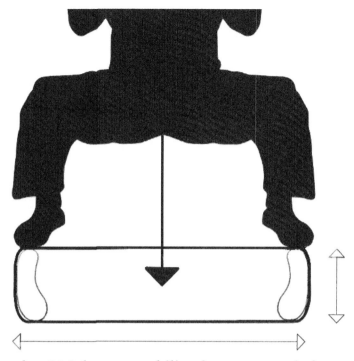

4. As the COG lowers stability increases as it becomes less and less likely for the line of gravity to move outside of the base. Imagine the increase in stability from a person standing, to kneeling, to quadruped (all fours), to lying flat on their belly or backs.

Influencing the stability and the balance of a human being is nothing more than influencing the relation of the line of gravity to their base. However, as we don't necessarily want to take the time to work out the exact location of the line of gravity we use the hypothetical COG mentioned above as easy reference.

To destabilise and unbalance a human being then is to move their COG outside of their base. When you understand this principle you understand two things: one, that all takedowns are essentially doing the same thing (moving the COG outside of the base); and two, that you don't need to know any specific takedown technique to actually facilitate a takedown. Improvisation becomes quick and easy. We'll cover this in more detail in a later chapter.

LINE OF STANCE INTEGRITY

The lines of stance integrity are imaginary lines drawn between a person's posts (load bearing assumed). This would always be the case irrespective of the individual's specific stance.

Consider for a moment a person standing flat footed, in this case the line of stance integrity would be an imaginary line from the one ankle to the other. **Observe a neutral and fighting stance as example below.**

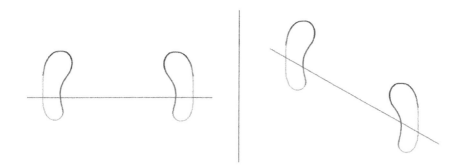

The same applies for someone down on all fours. **Even when using only the primary lines of stance integrity notice the more intricate lattice work on the left and how it changes when the person lifts up one hand from the floor.**

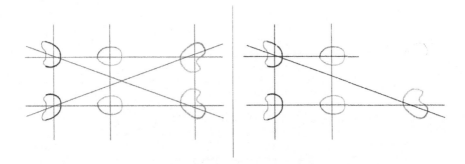

From a stability point of view, this line directly determines from which angles the person can receive applied force whilst still maintaining stability and balance. **For ease of learning, let's add a line in the center of the ankles from the first two sketches above. This first line is perpendicular to the line of stance integrity, creating four imaginary quadrants. Now let's shift those four quadrants by 45°**

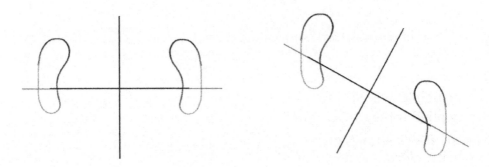

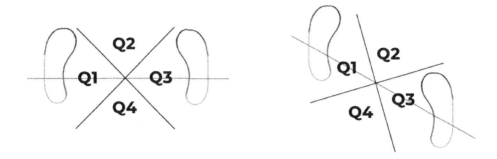

First note of importance, is that this person will only be able to receive applied force and maintain stability, within the angles contained in the two opposing quadrants in which the line of stance integrity falls (Q1 & Q3). Conversely, if the force is applied in the other two quadrants it will create instability and proceeding balance issues (Q2 & Q4). You can easily test this principle with a partner: push or shove each other around and note specifically how quickly one goes from stable to unstable once the force application crosses over from Q1 or Q3 into Q2 or Q4.

Furthermore, the larger the distance between the ankles the more force can be received from the stable angles and the less force can be received from unstable angles. Coinciding with this principle we can also add that the lower the recipient of the applied force's COG the more applied force can be received from the stable angles, albeit this relates back to the line of gravity now being closer to the ground.

It makes sense then, if one would wish to influence the stability of an opponent, whether simply aiming to destabilise/unbalance them, or to attempt a complete takedown, to do so from the unstable angles of attack, that is, from quadrants 2 or 4. Or in other words, to stay off their line of stance integrity.

We have two major options when it comes to unbalancing or affecting a takedown: one, we can create the instability in the opponent through varying tactics and techniques; or two, we can notice when the opponent has become unstable in and of their own movements, or possibly due to the dynamism of the actual close combat incident, and capitalise on that. (A close combat incident, or CCI for short, is defined as any incident that occurs within arms length, and that requires a combative application of force to resolve. It may be defensive or offensive in nature.)

We need to remember that existing instability, in this sense, relates to the opponent either being stationary but on the precipice of losing balance, or that they are moving in an unstable manner and trying to correct their balance during the movement. In both cases, less force would need to be applied to cause them to lose balance completely than if you were trying to create the instability yourself. It stands to reason, then, that it is easier to simply capitalise on the opponent's instability than to create it yourself. When we remain aware of an opponent's line of stance integrity, as well as how his movements correspond to it, it becomes easier to identify momentary instability and we can use that as opportunity to further destabilise them.

This, however, requires the practice of Continuous Assessment, defined in The Maul Book (Holloway and Coleman) as the mental discipline of continuously assessing various factors in a CCI whilst the CCI is still active. This discipline does not come naturally and should be actively developed.

COG ACCESS

The COG is best imagined as sitting in the lower trunk of the human body rather than in the pelvis. Should the hip hinge 90° to the front, it would sit on the segment now parallel to the floor and not the segment that is still upright. This means, that if we need to access the COG for the purpose of manipulation, we essentially need to access the lower trunk. We can do so directly, meaning by physically taking hold of that segment and manipulating it, or we can do so via the body's joints.

The joints in the human body are made up of two basic categories, or functions, of joints. There are mobilising joints and there are stabilising joints. **See the diagram below.**

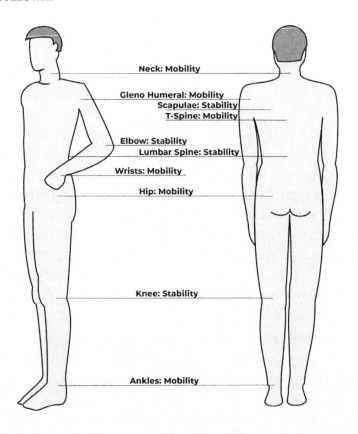

Neck: Mobility

Gleno Humeral: Mobility
Scapulae: Stability
T-Spine: Mobility

Elbow: Stability
Lumbar Spine: Stability

Wrists: Mobility

Hip: Mobility

Knee: Stability

Ankles: Mobility

In general, and when compared to stabilising joints, mobilising joints have a very high range of motion; most mobilising joints can move in multiple planes of movement and rotation, as well as through multiple degrees of angle. Stabilising joints, at most, can move through one plane of movement and are very restricted in terms of the angle, as well as range of motion.

In terms of the mobilising joints we have the neck (cervical spine), thoracic spine, wrists, gleno-humeral, hip and ankle joints. In terms of the stabilising joints we have the elbows, scapulae, lumbar spine and knee joints. It's a point of interest that joints are chained together mostly in opposing function. As discussed previously, the COG is estimated to sit in front of the second sacral joint, however, we will be ignoring the sacral spine for the purpose of this discussion.

Axiom: the closer we get to the lower trunk, the less joints there are between the point of applied force and the COG; the further away we move the more joints there are between the point of applied force and the COG.

For example, if we had to grab the opponent by the head, we only have the cervical, thoracic, and lumbar spine between the point of applied force and the lower trunk containing the COG. If we had to grab the opponent's upper arm we would need to add the gleno-humeral and scapular joint to the list. If we had to grab their lower arm we would need to add the elbow, and if we had to grab the opponent's hand we would need to add both the elbow and the wrist. If we had to go for the opponent's lower body, possibly grabbing their upper thigh, we only have the hip joint between the point of applied force and the COG. For the sake of thoroughness let's complete our distal journey: If you had to grab the opponent by the lower leg you would have the knee and the hip joint between the point of applied force and the COG, and if you had to grab them by the foot you would now have to add the ankle joint to the list.

There are two important points to take away from the above: one, the further away from the COG we apply force the more joints we have to deal with; and two, the joints are made to facilitate certain movements and, as such, those movements need to be accounted for and addressed to effectively influence the COG. What does this mean practically, though? It means I need to restrict the movement in the joint so that I can access the COG from a distal position. This can essentially only be done in three ways (of which all other methods are simply variations):

> 1. Applying force antagonistically to the joint's functional range of motion. Imagine a hyper extended elbow with force being applied directly to the back of the elbow.

> 2. Collapsing the joint and locking it into its fully flexed range of motion. Imagine a wrist or ankle lock being applied to a fully flexed elbow or knee joint.

3. Extending the joint to its natural end of range position. Imagine yanking someone on an already straight arm, with elbow fully extended, versus yanking them on a bent elbow. In the first case the extended elbow will give you access to the shoulder joint meaning the yank will affect the opponent's torso. In the second case the yank might simply straighten out the arm with no applied force reaching the opponent's torso.

All of this is important for the following reason: we are trying to apply force to the COG with the purpose of influencing the line of gravity in relation to the base. We are doing so to either create instability and loss of balance, or to affect a takedown. However, if you are not applying force directly to the COG then, as is more frequently the case, you are trying to do so through one or multiple joints. The potential problem, though, is that if you do not restrict or remove the movement capability from the joint or joints between the applied force and the COG, most or all of the force that is being applied will simply dissipate through the joints. We call this bleeding off.

Imagine for a moment a vehicle's shock absorber. You are holding it upright with the one end in your hands and the other against the floor. As you push down, the shock absorber simply absorbs the applied force; the applied force is bleeding off into the shock absorber's "joint" (btw, biomechanically speaking this is one of the purposes of our joints - to absorb incoming force; it assists with, for example, breaking falls or catching heavy or fast moving objects).

By now you should be understanding that if you do not account for the movement capability of the joints, then whatever force you apply will never fully reach the COG. Incidentally, this is why so many joint locks precede and/or form part of takedowns. It's the purpose of the joint locks to provide access to the COG. This is one of the essential breakdowns in most unsuccessful attempts at unbalancing or taking down an opponent. When you are attempting to unbalance or take down your opponent via one or more joints, always make sure the joint is properly locked before proceeding.

TAKEDOWNS

We now have sufficient understanding of the Fundamentals to properly consider takedowns. However, let's first consider one possible technical definition of a takedown.

A takedown is any technique that causes an opponent to fall by moving that opponent's line of gravity outside of their base.

When it comes to this, there are only four basic strategies that underpin all of the myriad of takedown techniques found across the martial and combative arts. It's axiomatic that each of these are essentially an interplay between the base and the center of gravity.

1.   **Manually move the COG outside of the base.** This strategy would include any takedown that either grabs a hold of the COG and moves it outside of the base, as well as any takedown where the COG is accessed via the upper torso or the joints and then moved outside of the base.

2.   **Collapse a post that's currently bearing load.** We should remember that it's only the load bearing posts that form a part of the base. When one is collapsed it changes the dimensions of the base and, in so doing, might purposefully or inadvertently have moved the line of gravity outside the base. This strategy then would include takedowns that focus on collapsing the knees or possibly elbows (when down on all fours and posting on the hands). Frequently some more applied force is required to complete the takedown. Think collapsing a knee from behind whilst simultaneously yanking the opponent's torso back.

3. **Remove a post from underneath the COG.** Essentially the same physics as above but related to sudden leg sweeping, tackling and severe trauma for example, a leg blowing up or being severed through a mechanical accident.

4. **Immobilise a post under a moving COG.** The easiest example here is to imagine someone running and tripping. Whilst running there is momentum present. However, the mechanics of running is keeping the COG over the legs (or, in other words, the moving base). Always remember that walking and running are essentially controlled falls. The individual is purposefully pushing their COG outside of their base but then moving the base back under the COG by stepping. However, when a leg is tripped the base gets frozen up whilst the momentum is still driving the COG outside of it. Another example would be when a person bends fully at the hip joint. The torso has its weight forward and on top of upper thighs making movement of the legs difficult. Should the COG start to move forward, losing balance to the front, the brain will automatically try and send a leg forward to increase the dimensions of the base. However, when the torso is fully bent to the front it is difficult to do so fully and/or in a timely manner.

Being a treatment on Fundamentals instead of techniques, the idea was to purposefully shy away from listing techniques themselves. Also, when considering the myriad of martial and combative arts in the market place, a list of techniques can easily become convoluted with semantical problems. The same technique can easily be called A in Karate, B in Judo, and C in Filipino Martial Arts. (Not to mention all the creative names being used by certain contemporary and very mystical combative and edged weapon movements.)

It might be an interesting study, for you as reader, to categorise your system's takedowns within these four different strategies

- especially if you come from more traditional martial arts. Whereas it'll give you a deeper level of insight into your art, it will also assist you in troubleshooting: when you understand the essential strategy of the technique it becomes much more apparent where breakdowns in the techniques might or are busy occurring. The value of this should be very apparent for instructors in terms of assisting their students as well.

When it comes to less traditional combative systems, which are usually more concerned with outcomes than with techniques, there is much value as well. First of all, understanding the Fundamentals of takedowns means one can more easily select fewer, but more robust, techniques, allowing for more scenario based training time (a need in professional training environments). It also becomes easier to drive the student to accomplish a specific outcome: telling a student to complete "Technique A" or "Technique B," which can sometimes have quite abstract names, now becomes simply "collapse the leg."

PART 2

Striking

STRIKING AS FORCE APPLICATION

The purpose of all striking, like all take downs, is to apply force to an object or, for the purpose of this treatment, to certain targets on another person's body. Force, in physics, is essentially a form of push or pull that, when exerted on an object, influences that object's motion. When applying force to any object one of four things can happen: the object on which force is being applied can accelerate, decelerate, change direction, and/or change shape.

With a takedown we apply force to another person with the purpose of influencing that person's motion and subsequent position. In this sense the applied force is affected primarily with the goal of accelerating and/or changing the direction of the opponent (to the floor if successful).

When it comes to striking an opponent, we are primarily concerned with creating acceleration and changing the shape of the opponent's relevant targets. In terms of creating acceleration, we are referring to the opponent's head snapping in any direction and causing them to lose consciousness (remember, medically speaking, loss of consciousness is any state in which a person is not 100% conscious). In terms of changing shape, we are referring to any and all pain and damage; when force is applied "more" or "faster" or "more acute" than which the target can receive whilst maintaining physical integrity (no change in shape), it results in pain and/or damage.

Another way to think about it is as follows: yes, with both takedowns and striking we are applying force. However, whereas the overarching goal might be the same (to disengage, incapacitate, control or arrest, kill depending on context and desired outcome), the road taken is different. Through striking and takedowns we might be climbing the same mountain, aiming for the same peak, but we are doing so via different paths. Some might refer to this as strategy. Even though we are climbing the mountain using two different paths striking frequently features in both. For example:

Striking can be used to assist in the four general strategies of takedowns.

- Pushing someone off balance (strategy 1),

- push or stop kicking the back of the knee (strategy 2),

- sweeping the legs (strategy 3) and

- tripping someone running past (strategy 4) are all forms of striking.

Apart from the above, as well as the very obvious routes of knocking an opponent out, or using pain and/or damage to influence the opponent's mobility, motivation, and/or consciousness, striking can be used more technically and acutely. Some examples might be:

- Striking to the side of the neck causing a temporary restriction in blood flow to the brain.

- Striking to any nerve cluster with enough force to temporarily override the information flow in the CNS.

- Striking to the eyes or airway causing the opponent's brain to try and fix these problems before continuing the close combat incident.

Considering all of these examples it should start to become clear that striking is simply the more accute application of force causing acceleration and/or change of shape in the relevant targets.

To strike more effectively, then, is again to perfect the

Fundamentals involved in applied force. The equation for calculating applied force is as follows:

Force = Mass x Acceleration

Acceleration is defined as the increase of velocity of an object during motion. It is a very easy concept to understand and, in terms of increasing the applied force, the easiest part of the equation to develop. For this reason, even though we will be mentioning acceleration occasionally during this treatment, the main focus will be on the increase of mass as that is the more technical aspect of increasing applied force.

BODY MOVEMENT

The Fundamental of body movement is the primary aspect relating to mass in the applied force equation. Specifically, body movement's primary concern is to increase the amount of mass within the equation. Body movement, although consisting of all three dynamics discussed in this chapter, is primarily dependant on correct sequencing of movement patterns during the strike. It asks the question: how do we move in such a way as to increase the mass behind the strike?

The average adult pitching velocity (or speed) in baseball is about 40 meters per second (roughly 142KPH) with an acceleration of 98 meters per second; the average adult bowling speed is about 8 meters per second with an acceleration of 18 meters per second. For the sake of simplifying this exercise, let's imagine that the duration for which the pitch and the bowl accelerates is the same. Consider for a moment these three different scenarios:

1. Throwing a 149g baseball, accelerating at 98 m/s2 = 15 N, at another person.

2. Throwing a 1.5kg bowling ball, accelerating at 18 m/s2 = 27 N, at another person.

3. Throwing a 1.5kg bowling ball, accelerating at 98 m/s2 = 147 N, at another person.

It doesn't take much insight or imagination to understand that scenario three will be the most damaging by far. Even though this example is contextually different from the topic at hand, it highlights what we are trying to achieve through good body movement: to increase the mass behind the strike while maintaining good acceleration. In this sense we can liken scenario 1 to a fighter simply swinging his arm around and scenario 3 to a fighter adept at getting more or most of his mass behind the strike. No person will be able to get all of his mass behind the strike, the goal is to get the highest amount of mass behind the strike. We refer to the actual mass behind the strike as being the effective mass in the strike.

To increase effective mass one has to have an understanding of the concept of kinetic chains, as well as have a focus on two other dynamics: synergistic planes of movement and, ultimately, the correct sequencing of movement patterns within any given technique.

Kinetic Chains

In the interest of this book's treatment being as concise as possible, let us simply refer to a kinetic chain as a sequence of movements where the partaking muscles and joints have a synergistic effect on each other. A kinetic chain would be general in the sense that it's the gross motor movements that underlie similar techniques. Consider that a straight punch, a deflection of an incoming strike, as well as a single arm push, all include an arm extension (opening of the elbow joint) kinetic chain. In the same way a stop kick, a push kick and front snap kick all include a leg extension (opening of the knee joint) kinetic chain. Both of these kinetic chains would also be dependent on a good hip drive - or posterior kinetic drive - for them to optimise effective mass. Without the hip drive the student will simply be swinging arms and legs around.

Unfortunately it is outside the scope of this book to list all of the different kinetic chains and how they pertain to combatives and martial arts. A good introductory treatment that I have in my own library is "The Anatomy of Martial Arts by Dr. Norman Link and Lily Chou." There are a couple of more thorough treatments than "The Anatomy of Martial Arts" but it's a topic that can easily (and almost unnecessarily) be overdeveloped, as such I deem "The

Anatomy of Martial Arts" to be sufficient for most practitioners.

Planes of Movement

The human body has three primary planes of movement. To simplify we can relate these planes to basic directions of movement: the Sagittal plane, which relates to forward and backwards movement; the Lateral plane, which relates to side to side movement; and the Transverse plane, which relates to rotational movement. **See the illustration below:**

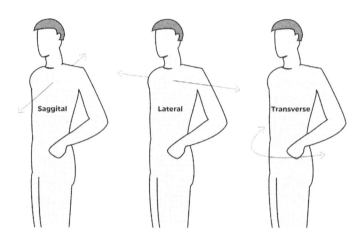

Increasing effective mass is dependant on synergistic motion related to the different planes of movement. A good straight punch (sagittal arm extension), for example, is more effective when flowing from a good hip drive (transverse). A good hip drive (transverse) can be enhanced by an explosive forward burst from a rear foot (sagittal leg extension).

When we break down a strike into these sequential movement patterns we will be able to notice how the different kinetic chains are stitched together into the complete technique. Each kinetic chain functions on a primary plane of movement. It's important to understand and identify these as any corrective action needs to be applied within the inherent plane of movement.

Another way of putting this is to say that we can draw a line of energy through the strike. Each kinetic chain, when achieved on the correct plane of movement, will increase the effective mass within the applied force.

Sequencing of Movement Patterns

The last component in increasing effective mass relates to the correct sequencing of movement patterns. This section will sound like simple common sense but it's our experience that many practitioners aren't even aware of either the glaring or the slight errors made in sequencing.

A good sequence of movements will almost always launch from a stable base. In terms of the base, one of the load carrying limbs, usually a leg, will initiate the technique. This is important as many practitioners initiate strikes with their torsos, hands, or arms, essentially crippling the increase of effective mass. From the the initial foot to leg drive there is a transfer of force that needs to happen through the hips either into the opposite leg or, through a stable core, into the upper torso. From the upper torso the drive will be completed through whichever body part the technique aims to do so. This can be the upper torso, either arm, elbow, lower arm, hand, etc., or possibly through the neck and head.

Because we're discussing mass in this chapter, imagine for a moment the comic of a snowball thrown down a hill: as it rolls down the hill it gathers more and more snow, increasing it's mass. When executing body movement correctly, we are adding mass to the "snowball" with every synergistic movement throughout the technique. Using the kinetic chains, in the correct planes of movement, and through the correct sequence of movement patterns, is what adds effective mass into the force equation.

STRUCTURE

If body movement is about increasing effective mass, structure is about ensuring that said mass gets "delivered." Structure is about the correct alignment of joints so that the force can actually travel through or down the kinetic chains described in the previous chapter. Joints that aren't correctly aligned throughout the kinetic chain causes a loss, or a bleeding off, of force.

For the treatment of this book we will think about structure in terms of absolutes: you either have structure or you don't. Technically this isn't accurate as there will always be some bleeding through every joint involved. However, our goal is always to minimise this bleeding and thinking in terms of absolutes assist in this process. It's important to remember one of the functions of certain joints is actually to act like shock absorbers. This allows us to reduce the force of impact when, for example, falling or being tackled by someone. This paragraph in the chapter titled COG Access applies:

> *Imagine for a moment a vehicle's shock absorber. You are holding it upright with the one end in your hands and the other against the floor. As you push down the shock absorber simply absorbs the applied force; the applied force is bleeding off into the shock absober's "joint" (BTW. This is one of the Fundamental purposes of our joints - to absorb incoming energy.)*

Reverse Engineering Structure

Reverse engineering structure allows us to find the joint positions in which we have structure. It's easier to reverse engineer certain strikes than others. Understanding the process, though, sheds light on both the Fundamental of structure as well as how we can develop it.

This would be the setup to analyse structure for a left handed straight punch:

1. Place the left fist against a wall making sure to pick a point of aim as you would when punching someone in the face.

2. Ensure only the desired knuckles of the fist are making contact with the wall.

3. Extend the arm just short of complete extension of the elbow.

4. Adjust first the torso and then the hips to ensure that the fist and extended arm are all aligned accordingly to the technique's ideal form.

5. Adjust the base to the hips.

6. If you are doing this exercise solo push as hard as you can into your fist. If you are assisting someone, you can push against their torso from behind.

What you are looking for is movement in any of the joints. Different striking techniques would obviously be projecting more or less force into certain joints. If we consider this left handed straight punch as an example, and assuming it's been set up properly, most of the bleeding tends to happen either in the wrist or the elbow. As such, you will see flexion or extension on the wrist and/or flexion on the elbow. As soon as you notice this you know there isn't structure and you need to adjust joint alignment until you find a position that has structure. The same would apply to all other joints involved in the kinetic chain.

When you have structure there will only be a slight compression on all the joints in involved in the specific technique. Nothing more.

Common Issues Related to Structure

Because of the general bleeding of force present in every strike we are left with an interesting dichotomy: the less joints involved in the body movement the more effective mass we are able to generate. This is due to the fact that we are removing some of the shock absorbers from the technique. Most of the mass comes into the force equation through adding the hips, trunk, and torso to the technique. When we remove distal joints we are increasing the ability of that mass to be successfully delivered.

However, the more joints present in the body movement the more acceleration or velocity we can generate. For example, elbows usually strike harder than hammerfists but the hammerfists has a higher acceleration at the end of the movement pattern. It is, however, possible to bleed of force in both of these examples if one doesn't have structure. Tactically this allows us different options when it comes to issues like range and/or outcome. All of that said, let's consider the most common issues related to structure:

• **There are three common indicators that there is no structure in the wrist or foot.** The first two relate to over extension or flexion of the joint, evidenced in the common wrist or foot strain or sprain when punching or kicking. The third, more dominant in striking with the fist, relates to losing skin on the knuckles; you lose the skin of your knuckles either because you are not aiming well, or because the joint is flexing and causing your knuckles to slip of the target. This can most frequently be identified by punching a bag without any protection. If you are losing skin on your knuckles the solution isn't to wear protection - it's to find out why you aren't punching straight into the bag.

• **When striking with the hands, or kicking distal of the knee, force bleeds off when the elbow or knee isn't appropriately extended.** This dynamic is evidenced clearly when reverse engineering structure in related techniques. It is mostly a question of incorrect range and this aspect will be addressed in the next chapter. The result is very simply that much of the force will bleed off through the joint and in whichever direction the proximal part of the limb is pointing upon impact.

- **When striking with an elbow it tends to bleed off force when it's not fully flexed upon impact.** Remember flexing is the act of closing a joint. When the elbow joint isn't fully closed upon impact the open elbow simply absorbs the force upon impact. A tight and compact elbow is required upon impact.

RANGE

All weapons have an effective range; there is a specific range in which every weapon is the most effective. Once we move outside of a weapon's effective range it starts losing efficacy. Whereas firearms, for example, have dynamic ranges at which they are very effective (think pistols from point blank up until about 10 - 15 meters), our striking weapons or techniques actually have very static effective ranges. Your arm is only so long and this essentially determines the range for a punch, hammer fist, palm strike, etc. I can adjust the range using footwork and body movement, but I can't adjust the length of the arm. In this way all of our striking weapons have essentially limited, static ranges.

It is the work of the practitioner to become the master of their own range. Understanding exactly how far one can and subsequently have to strike from is not only an invaluable skill in close combat but also a Fundamental in force application.

Where the weapons in close combat have a static range, the range between combatants themselves is dynamic. Apart from the fact that we need to master our own range we also need to master the dynamism or range between ourselves and our opponents. Effective force delivery is dependant on me reading the range between myself and my opponent and selecting the correct weapon for that range. This order is important. We always choose the correct weapon for the range. **Review this table before we proceed:**

WEAPON	RANGE
Head and Shoulders	Extreme Close Range
Elbows and Knees	Short Range
Hands and Forearms	Medium Range
Legs	Long Range

Patching the Range

When we choose a weapon whose range is too short to reach the target the brain will frequently try to patch the range by closing (decreasing the distance) on the target. However, the patch work is most frequently achieved by leaning towards with the torso instead of adjusting the base (moving the feet). This happens for two reasons: one, the feet are the base of the technique and as such the brain perceives the need to keep them anchored to the surface from which it is driving; and two, it is much easier and faster to simply move the torso than the whole body. Seeing as striking usually happens with high acceleration and/or at high velocity the brain's quickest adjustment for range is to simply lean in. This is also one of the primary reasons why the brain will initiate the chaotic flailing of the arms instead of striking purposefully when it comes to a frenzied CCI: the arms are even more mobile, faster, and available than the torso.

The problem with the above is that the brain is now moving the COG closer or over the base at speeds at which it is difficult to correct the proceeding stability issues. This can frequently be seen when a fighter reaches for a punch and either loses balance or very easily gets moved off balance by their opponent.

Breaking the Structure

On the opposite side of the spectrum we have a weapon whose range is longer than the distance between the practitioner and the opponent.

As example consider the opponent being in extreme close range, where a head butt would be the correct weapon, deploying an elbow. Alternatively, the opponent might be in short range, calling for an elbow, but deploying a straight punch.

In any situation where a weapon with a longer range than the distance between opponents is deployed it would be impossible to have structure. When this happens most of the force will simply bleed off through the joint that does not have structure. It will do so in the direction that the limb proximal to the joint in question is pointing.

Ranging

I start off all new clients with a reverse engineering process we call ranging. I also use ranging to problem solve. Ie. When we are running into force delivery issues we will stop and range to confirm that it's not the range creating the problem. The process of ranging is very similar to that of finding structure described in the previous chapter. The setup would be exactly the same - meaning to start from the weapon and reverse engineer it all the way to the base. The goal however is not to test for structure but simply to find correct foot placement for the base.

One main difference is that we would range on a dynamic target and not a wall. When finding structure we want to push against an immovable object so that we see the bleed. When ranging we need to be mindful of where we are actually striking to. For example, with a straight punch I am actually striking into my opponent: ideally about two to three inches. Therefore, it makes more sense to range on an opponent or a punching bag so that you can place the weapon two to three inches into the target and range from there on backwards.

FORCE DELIVERY DYNAMICS

Let's start with an axiom: force is applied through contact.

Here we are not referring to the result of the force being applied (acceleration, deceleration, change in direction, change in shape), but rather to what is happening to the force itself when making contact. It is the nature of the contact to influence "how" the force is applied. For this reason, we will be referring to this as force delivery dynamics. There are four main factors that influence force delivery:

1. Contact duration between the weapon and the target.

2. Surface area of the weapon.

3. Sharp edges and/or points.

4. Blunt weapons.

Contact Duration

The longer a weapon remains in contact with the target the slower the force delivery. This essentially changes the type of strike. For example, when considering the hands as weapons, long contact would be a push or a shove, short contact would be an impact strike like a punch or an elbow. In terms of the feet long contact might be a push- or defensive kick with short contact being a quick stop or snap kick. In both examples it is the same amount of force generated but the contact duration changes what actual strike it becomes upon delivery.

An important principle to understand then is that contact

duration determines how much of the generated force is delivered within the contact timeframe. This is important as, with impact striking like punching and elbows and so forth, we obviously want to deliver as much force as possible upon impact. However, should you strike and maintain contact for longer than necessary this will have a negative impact on how much force is delivered upon impact.

There is a skill then to develop in terms of landing a powerful strike at the correct range and with structure: but then to reset the weapon as fast as possible. This ensures that the maximum amount of force is delivered upon first contact. The easiest way to think about resetting a weapon in striking is simply to reset back to the required fighting stance.

It's also important not to reset the weapon too quickly; when we reset the weapon too quickly we might be short striking, essentially just "tapping" the opponent instead of properly delivering the intended force. At the risk of eliciting some critique certain light contact styles of sport fighting (like JKA Karate for example) are prone to this error.

Surface Area

The larger the surface area of the weapon the less concentrated the delivery of force. There is a slight correlation between increased surface area and slower contact duration and decreased surface area and faster contact duration. This is evidenced when considering shoving someone with the hands or affecting a defensive push kick, both techniques have longer contact times whilst also using the weapons complete surface area. Conversely, when considering a bare knuckle punch, preferably only making contact with the knuckles of the index and middle finger, or a snap kick to the solar plexus using only the ball of the foot, both techniques are supposed to have short contact times whilst using significantly less of the weapon's surface area.

When aiming to apply force more acutely, usually with the intention of increasing the possibility of pain and damage, the practitioner needs to mindful of striking with the smaller and intended surface area of the weapon.

Edge and Point

Building on the previous point we can now understand why sharp and pointed objects so easily penetrate, lacerate, and/or damage the human body. Essentially all of the force behind the weapon is concentrated and delivered either through the sharp edge or the point.

Marc MacYoung made a good argument, to which I agree, that knives specifically should be referred to as strike enhancers and not force multipliers. A force multiplier suggests that I'm somehow generating or delivering more force. This might be the case with large edged or pointed weapons, those with significant mass, but not so with knives.

When using an edged or pointed weapon I am primarily changing how acutely the force is delivered as well as altering and/or enhancing its terminal delivery dynamics.

Blunt Weapons

When considering blunt weapons we can also draw on what we learned in the chapter about structure. Essentially a blunt weapon combines the issue of structure with that of contact duration and/or surface area. By this we mean to say that most blunt weapons have total structure; unless the weapon changes shape or breaks (which is also a form of changing shape) there is no bleeding of force. There might still be a bleeding of force in the practitioners body movement but the blunt weapon itself maintains integrity upon impact. This ensures that the force generated gets delivered in an optimal way.

Blunt weapons can be considered both as force multipliers and strike enhancers. The increases in effective force might not be as much with all types of blunt weapons but generally blunt weapons intrinsically add mass to the equation. In the case of large blunt weapon that have quite a bit of mass (like a baseball bat or a sledgehammer) the increase in effective mass is quite high. Conversely, hasty blunt weapons like a book or a tv remote might have a negligible effect on effective mass. All blunt weapons aim, though, to enhance the strike through providing structure to the weapon upon impact.

DID YOU ENJOY THIS BOOK?

The best way to thank an author for writing a book you enjoyed is to leave an honest review! If you are reading on paper you can do so by heading back to the page you purchased this book from. Alternatively, select the link below to post your review of 'Schalk's Little Book on Fundamentals'.

Thank you so much for taking the time to let other readers know what you thought of my book!

(PS. I sincerely love photos of books - and photos of my own books all the more! :D If you have any feel free to share one with me on social media; I'll be sure to post it and then credit you!)

Click here to review.

FOLLOW SCHALK TO KEEP UPDATED

facebook.com/schalkhollowayauthor

instagram.com/schalkhollowayauthor

amazon.com/author/schalkholloway

www.schalkholloway.com

Schalk is a South African author known for The Maul Book, Schalk's Little Book Series, and Die Groot Storie. Schalk started his career as novelist in 2022 after suffering and recovering from a serious injury. His first novels, the Brooklyn Saga, drew inspiration from the years that he ran interventions in that tiny Cape Town suburb.

Schalk's professional background lies in Christian ministry, combatives and firearms instruction, as well as tactical and intelligence based operations in select security and policing environments (references available upon request).

OTHER BOOKS BY SCHALK

NOVELS

The Brooklyn Saga:

Disciple's Fault
Brother's Request

SUBJECT LITERATURE

The Maul Book (co-authored with Gavin Coleman)

The Little Book Series:

Schalk's Little Book on Fundamentals (The Black Book)
Schalk's Little Book of Combative Principles (The White Book)
Schalk's Little Book for Brothers (The Red Book)

Disciple's Fault on Amazon

Frank Night is a lay minister that spends all his free time running interventions in at-risk communities. When the tiny community of Brooklyn, Cape Town, offers him two new cases, an unconventional stabbing leading to the death of a local boy, and a self-mutilating girl that disappears one Saturday night, he suddenly finds himself with much to do and manage.

A diagnosed neuro-divergent, his interactions with others are strained and complex at the best of times. But when the stress from these two interventions, as well as what seems like a neighbourhood that's set itself against him, starts to mount, he finally loses control. Just for an instant he becomes the man he used to be. Unfortunately for them, that single misstep places his wife firmly in the crosshairs of one of the local monsters.

REVIEW:

"Schalk's background gives him a huge edge when it comes to details and visualizations. The story is incredible and though written like a novel I get subtle hints that most of this book was written with experience. This is a great read and gives you a small slice of the pie in the combative world and life in Cape Town." - Loni Young

Brother's Request on Amazon

It's a couple of months after that disturbing night in Brooklyn. Frank and Didi have just started settling down but Brooklyn and the community's at it again: Jenny brings over a silent and highly detached friend, a new prostitute starts working their corner, and whereas Hamma's eventually finding his feet, certain interactions between him and the community has Frank concerned.

As if all of that isn't enough, even while Frank's trying to manage his neuro-divergence, he's also realising that he might slowly be losing control. Half the time he can't sleep due to nightmares and the other half is dominated by his recurring flashbacks. To complicate matters even further: a ghost from his past arrives in the neighbourhood.

A formidable man, and one that he used to call brother.

The Maul Book on Amazon

Did you know that the latest technology and research shows that the brain undergoes very specific changes in its functioning during a close combat incident? Whether training for self defence, law enforcement / military close combat procedures, or traditional martial arts and sports fighting - under certain conditions the brain will switch from one mode of functioning to another. The Maul Book is the first book to delve into this research, and through extensive testing within different close combat environments, integrate this research into new and fresh training methodologies. The Maul book is a must for any practitioner from any martial arts, self defence, close combat or tactical environment, as well as for instructors serious about providing the best training developed and influenced through the latest research.

Here's what you will learn from The Maul Book:

• What the latest research teaches on the brain's functioning under certain conditions.

• Old brain models that have now been shown as defunct and obsolete.

• How the changes in brain function influences performance and decision making within highly dynamic environments.

• How to better identify and select targets within high speed and ever changing situations.

• Techniques, tactics and training methodologies that work WITH the brain and its different ways of functioning.

• How to apply this research into any martial art or close combat system.

core knowledge base of The Maul as an example of how to grate the research into an existing system.

VIEWS:

"I could easily just state that this is one of the best books on knife combatives I have read, ever, and be done with it. But that would be a disservice to both the authors and to you, the reader… It is, quite simply, the best approach to realistic knife combatives written in years… I cannot give it a higher recommendation than this, read it, practice it, read it again, and keep working it. This is good stuff. I wish this book was out when I started in this arena." - Terry Trahan

"The Maul tells you why some things probably won't work and why you should reassess your own training to realign it with what is currently known about the human brain. This is the most important book on Defensive Edged Weapons to come out in years." - Don Rearic

Schalk Holloway

Schalk's Little Book of Combative Principles on Amazon

Combatives, both in the sense of a set of techniques as well as a complete system, runs on very specific principles. These principles differ significantly from traditional martial arts and sport fighting systems. Most frequently combatives are applied within combat, law enforcement, security or self defense contexts. This means that the risk of severe injury or death is ever present. When we don't understand or incorporate true combative principles into our training we run the risk of losing within a context where losing can cost us our lives.

In this Little Book:

• The 3 main contextual considerations when it comes to combatives training and development.

• The importance of understanding your context and the factors that are influenced by context.

• Introduction to the Combative Triad.

• The core principles for successfully managing close combat incidents.

• Considerations on what needs to be included in training to successfully incorporate these principles.

The "Schalk's Little Book Series" is a collection of concise treatments on certain martial arts and combative related themes and topics. All the books are just under 10 000 words in length and purposefully designed to be easily digested and referenced.

/:

ı time I read a new title by Schalk, I get happy, because good,
ıl information is about to get in the hands of people that need
ſhese "Little Books" are extremely valuable, and written in a
:ry concise yet readable style. The newest one in your hands now,
ﬁives a very good overview of the training principles that really
are universal, and important to successfully navigating the real
world use of Combatives. There is no fluff between these covers,
no padding of the lessons, just like Combatives, they are short, to
the point, and if understood and trained, give you great bang for
your buck. There is also plenty of room in this short book to work
and wrestle with the lessons, to really make them yours, and apply
them. I can't recommend this enough. Good, usable, concise, well
presented, and accurate. This is a book you will keep going back to,
as your eyes open, and your understanding grows." - Terry Trahan

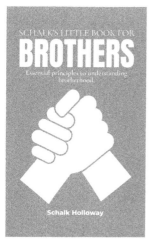

Schalk's Little Book for Brothers on Amazon

For many of us, the concept of brotherhood was entrenched (pun intended) in the literal and proverbial trenches.

Whether on the streets, in the military or other teams, or through the navigation of large societal chaos or deep personal adversity, a relationship was tested by fire and found to be gold: men, or women, were brought together, almost as if destined or divinely appointed, to face life, death, and all the tragic adversity in between, together.

However, the word is complex: for some it means I've killed for you, or I've almost been killed for you, and I'll do it again; for others it stands almost next to nothing, an empty term, meaning no more than: 'Hey, you.'

This Little Book is an attempt to concisely unpack and highlight the principles that underlie true brotherhood. If it's successful it might help some of us understand the word in a more healthy and balanced manner, and it might help some others, at the very least, to be more careful when they use the word, but hopefully, to know that when they do use it, that it should actually mean something.

The "Schalk's Little Book Series" is a collection of concise treatments on certain martial arts and combative related themes and topics. All the books are just under 10 000 words in length and purposefully designed to be easily digested and referenced.

Printed in Great Britain
by Amazon

19456105R00041